SHADOWS OF SCANDAL

The Unsettling World of Jeffrey Epstein, Ghislaine Maxwell, Harvey Weinstein And the Enigma That Lies Behind Closed Doors

By

Cassandra T. Peters

TABLE OF CONTENT

Jeffrey Epstein was a banker and convicted sex offender who became well-known for his associations with various influential persons, such as politicians, celebrities, and business executives, inside elite social circles. Ghislaine Maxwell, a British socialite, is the daughter of media tycoon Robert Maxwell. Maxwell maintained a strong association with Epstein over an extended period and was frequently referred to as his confidante. She was accused of participating in Epstein's illicit sex trafficking activities, including engaging in the recruitment and manipulation of underage females for him and other individuals. Harvey Weinstein, formerly a prominent figure in Hollywood, saw his career come to an end as a result of multiple accusations of sexual harassment and assault. Some of these allegations resulted in legal charges and subsequent convictions.

Shadows of Scandal is an enthralling exploration of the depths of depravity, delving into the scandalous narratives surrounding the lives, professional trajectories, and legal proceedings of Jeffrey Epstein, Ghislaine Maxwell, and Harvey Weinstein. This terrifying revelation uncovers the dynamics of power, deceit, the secretive realms of the privileged class and the hidden aspects of their existence, shedding light on a world where privilege and perversion mix, from their influential ties to the infamous private island.

The cautionary tales surrounding Epstein, Maxwell, and Weinstein compel society to confront unsettling realities regarding the misuse of authority and the frequently intricate journey towards retribution. Inevitably, the enduring consequences of these cases will shape the ongoing dialogue concerning sexual abuse and the quest for justice amidst entrenched power structures.

CHAPTER ONE

Early Life and Career of Jeffrey Epstein

Jeffrey Epstein, an American individual, was born on January 20, 1953 in Brooklyn, New York, U.S. Epstein was involved in serial sex trafficking, pedophilia, and finance. Epstein amassed a substantial fortune and cultivated a network of affluent individuals, influential politicians, and even members of royalty through his prosperous financial career. Ultimately, he faced allegations of orchestrating an extensive enterprise involved in human trafficking, wherein he and his accomplices obtained women and girls for the purpose of engaging in sexual activities with him and his privileged acquaintances. Epstein passed away in 2019 while incarcerated and anticipating a federal prosecution for sex trafficking.

Where it all began...

Epstein was the eldest of two offspring born to Paula Epstein and Seymour Epstein, both of whom were descendants of Jewish immigrants. His mother was a housewife, while his father was employed as a groundskeeper and gardener for the New York City Parks Department. The family resided in Sea Gate, a middle-class neighborhood in Brooklyn, which is located on the western coast of Coney Island. Epstein demonstrated exceptional aptitude in mathematics, showcasing his talent as a highly accomplished student. In addition, he possessed exceptional piano-playing abilities. He enrolled at Lafayette High School in Gravesend, Brooklyn, where the majority of the student population consisted of Italian Americans. Epstein is believed to have encountered instances of anti-Semitism during his time there. He completed his education in 1969, after advancing two grades. Subsequently, he matriculated in the Cooper Union for the Advancement of Science and Art, where he pursued his studies until 1971. in that point, he relocated to the Courant Institute of Mathematical Sciences at New York University (NYU). He attended New York University for a duration of three years but did not successfully complete his studies.

In 1974, Epstein commenced instructing physics and mathematics at the exclusive Dalton School in Manhattan, although without an academic degree. Notably, a significant portion of the school's student body hailed from affluent families in the nation. Epstein exhibited inappropriate behavior while he was employed at Dalton. As an illustration, he purportedly attended a gathering for high-school kids, where he shown excessive attention towards females—although he was not charged with any form of sexual misconduct at that particular moment.

In 1976, Epstein made such a strong impression on a student's father during a parent-teacher conference that the father recommended Epstein to Alan ("Ace") Greenberg, the CEO of Bear Stearns, a prominent Wall Street financial firm, who also happened to be a parent at Dalton. After the 1975–76 school year, Epstein was fired from his post at Dalton due to an evaluation that revealed no improvement in his teaching abilities. Shortly thereafter, he commenced his employment at Bear Stearns.

Partner at Bear Stearns and CEO

J. Epstein & Company

In 1976, Epstein resigned from his teaching position to join the firm. During Epstein's time at Dalton, his potential for a successful finance career started to flourish. Epstein became a limited partner at Bear Stearns in 1980, four years after entering the company. Nevertheless, in 1981, he departed from the organization to establish his own enterprise. Around this period, Epstein's personal financial circumstances, as well as his business methods, started to become more ambiguous. During the

1980s, some individuals who were connected to him claimed that he identified himself as a "bounty hunter" who retrieved stolen funds on behalf of the extremely affluent. Epstein commenced his collaboration with Steve Hoffenberg, an executive at Towers Financial Corporation, in 1987. The duo made endeavors, albeit largely unsuccessful, in their pursuits of company acquisitions.

In 1988, Epstein established J. Epstein & Company, a consultancy that offered financial management services to clients possessing a net worth over $1 billion. For about two decades, his primary customer was the affluent retail tycoon Leslie Wexner. Epstein assumed control over a significant portion of Wexner's assets and profited immensely as a consequence.

During the 1990s, Epstein commenced operating his business from the island of St. Thomas in the U.S. Virgin Islands, which is recognized as a tax haven. Additionally, he possessed the neighboring island of Little St. James. Subsequently, he acquired a further island in close proximity, namely Great St. James. In addition, he possessed the largest private residence in Manhattan at that time, along with estates in Palm

Beach, Florida; Paris; and New Mexico. Epstein allegedly utilized concealed surveillance devices at his Manhattan abode to capture sexual activities carried out by his affluent acquaintances, likely with the intention of using the recordings for blackmail. In addition, he maintained a record of individuals who journeyed on his personal aircraft, known among the residents of the Virgin Islands as the "Lolita Express" due to its association with Vladimir Nabokov's novel Lolita (1955), in which the protagonist is a middle-aged man who has an intense and unhealthy desire for underage girls. The individuals included in the list were former U.S. president Bill Clinton, Donald Trump, the distinguished attorney and Harvard University law professor Alan Dershowitz, and Prince Andrew, duke of York, who was ultimately accused of engaging in sexual activity with one of Epstein's juvenile victims on multiple occasions.

In 2002, Epstein gained prominence as an individual who cultivated relationships with influential and renowned individuals, and became widely recognized for financially supporting a journey to Africa involving President Bill and the actors Kevin

Spacey and Chris Tucker to Africa via a specially modified private aircraft for the purpose of seeing AIDS project locations. In 2003, he collaborated with film mogul Harvey Weinstein in an unsuccessful attempt to acquire New York magazine. Coincidentally, during the same year, he generously donated $30 million to Harvard University. The purpose of this donation was to create a program focused on mathematical biology and evolutionary dynamics. The donation showcased Epstein's prominent affiliations, as he received public praise from Alan Dershowitz, a distinguished Harvard professor at the time. Dershowitz later played a role in Epstein's legal representation during his 2007 sex crimes allegations. The donation became part of what some perceived as Epstein's meticulously orchestrated endeavors to cultivate an image of himself as a distinguished individual.

However, he made a conscious effort to maintain his privacy, allegedly avoiding social gatherings and dining at restaurants. He had romantic relationships with women such as Eva Andersson Dubin, who won the Miss Sweden competition, and Ghislaine Maxwell, the daughter of publisher

Robert Maxwell. However, he never entered into matrimony.

Epstein's deliberate connection to Clinton appeared intentional, as he stated in 2002 that his exclusive social network was a "portfolio" that he actively cultivated. "I allocate my resources towards individuals, whether it be in the realm of politics or science," Epstein stated. "That is my area of expertise."

Despite the lack of clarity regarding the precise means by which Epstein accumulated his wealth, his financial resources began to have a global impact as he acquired properties worldwide and established a foundation that made donations to Harvard University.

Epstein's charitable endeavors reached their peak with the establishment of the Jeffrey Epstein VI Foundation. Epstein has not only had a friendly relationship with Clinton, but also with other presidents. Donald Trump and Epstein were part of the same social circles, and it appears that Trump was aware from an early stage of the well-known fact that Epstein frequently had young ladies around him.

In 2002, real-estate tycoon Donald Trump characterized Epstein to a magazine as an individual who takes pleasure in his social activities and has a preference for ladies who are very young. "I have been acquainted with Jeff for a duration of fifteen years," Trump stated to the magazine during that period. "Exceptional individual." He is quite enjoyable to spend time with. It is rumored that he shares my appreciation for attractive ladies, particularly those who are younger.

CHAPTER TWO

Ghislaine Maxwell's Early Life

Ghislaine Maxwell, the youngest of nine children, was born on Christmas Day 1961 in Maisons-Laffitte, a prosperous town in northern France. She is the daughter of Robert Maxwell, a British newspaper magnate, and his French wife Elisabeth. Her adolescent sibling Michael was engaged in a vehicular collision that resulted in an extended state of unconsciousness until his demise in 1967, a calamity that deeply impacted the family. Ghislaine and her siblings grew up in Oxford, specifically at the Maxwells' Headington Hill Hall residence. This expansive mansion also functioned as the base for their father's Pergamon Press publishing company. At the age of 14, Ghislaine contributed to the company by acquiring programming skills to operate a new set of Wang computers that her father had implemented in 1973 as part of a modernization effort.

According to reports, the Maxwell siblings were subjected to strict standards by their father. He would frequently summon them sternly to discuss their future aspirations in the presence of his distinguished guests during dinners at Headington. While some of the siblings rejected this atmosphere, Ghislaine described it as "inspiring" in an interview. Maxwell enrolled at Marlborough College and Balliol College, Oxford, where she pursued a degree in modern history with a focus on languages.

During her time there, she formed a friendship with the actor Hugh Grant and founded an Oxford United supporters club. Eventually, she took on a role as a director of the football club after her father assumed the position of chairman from 1982 to 1987. Ghislaine Maxwell gained recognition as a prominent figure in high society during the 1980s. She often traveled as a consultant for her father's companies and managed a corporate gifts business that he established specifically for her.

The Strange Passing of Robert Maxwell

On the evening of November 5, 1991, a Spanish fisherman observed the corpse of Robert Maxwell, the contentious British media mogul, drifting in the Atlantic Ocean close to the Canary Islands. The crew of Maxwell's opulent motor yacht had spent the whole day scouring for him, following his unexplained disappearance earlier that morning. Conspiracy theories arose almost instantaneously. Possible culprits speculated upon were operatives from a group of underwater commandos from the Mossad. Supporting this notion, it was noted that Maxwell had long been speculated to have connections with multiple intelligence organizations. Perhaps he was silenced to prevent him from divulging sensitive information.

Despite the presence of a more straightforward and compelling reason for Maxwell's death, a few individuals persist in adhering to these fabrications. Upon embarking on his yacht, he was aware that his business empire, Maxwell

Communication Corporation, which he had dedicated decades to constructing, was on the verge of collapse due to overwhelming debt. Additionally, he was aware that, in a futile attempt to avoid this result, he and his colleagues had embezzled hundreds of millions of pounds from M.C.C.'s employee pensions and utilized the funds to artificially bolster the company's stock value. As a result, the remaining Maxwell family and the British government became responsible for this debt.

Following the unavoidable declaration of bankruptcy, this illicit scheme would come to light. Maxwell would face severe consequences, including reputational damage, disgrace, and a high probability of incarceration. For a man who was consumed by excessive pride and deep-seated insecurity, despite his fame on two continents, the idea of facing financial collapse and public disgrace was unbearable. This was the same year he acquired the Daily News. Consequently, he leaped off the ship and into the water. Maxwell's demise is surrounded by uncertainties, including the absence of a suicide note and the inability of a group of coroners to reach a definitive conclusion regarding the cause of death. This leaves room for the possibility of a heart attack or accidental drowning.

In June 1992, Ghislaine's brothers, Ian and Kevin, were apprehended and accused of fraud. However, they were subsequently cleared of all charges in January 1996.

The Epstein-Maxwell Saga

The motor yacht upon which Maxwell made his last strides was named Lady Ghislaine. Following his demise, Ghislaine Maxwell relocated to New York, where she encountered Epstein and subsequently entered into a romantic relationship with him. According to certain reports, she also assumed the role of procuring individuals for him. (She has vehemently refuted these allegations.)

Similar to Maxwell, Epstein was a self-made individual who originated from Coney Island and did not have a college degree, yet relied on his intelligence and resourcefulness. Similar to Maxwell, he actively sought the favor of influential individuals, despite the unclear origins of his wealth. In 1995, Epstein, following the example of Ghislaine's father, established a new business called the Ghislaine Corporation, headquartered in Palm Beach, Florida. However, the venture was unsuccessful and was disbanded three years later.

Subsequent civil court cases against Epstein would later claim that it was during the mid-1990s when he initially encountered several underage girls who would later accuse him of sexual abuse. These girls include an unnamed 13-year-old music student and two teenage sisters, Marie and Annie Farmer. Marie, a talented visual artist, was approached by Epstein at a New York art gallery after he showed interest in one of her paintings.

In 1999, Maxwell is believed to have initially met Virginia Giuffre while living at Epstein's residence in Florida. Giuffre, who would later accuse the billionaire of sexual assault in January 2015, was a minor employed at the Mara-Lago club owned by Donald Trump at that time. In 2000, Maxwell relocated to a townhouse in New York, which was conveniently close to Epstein's property. Both Maxwell and Epstein were invited to a social event at the Queen's Sandringham House estate in Norfolk by their mutual friend, Prince Andrew. It is worth noting that Prince Andrew had previously been photographed with Ms. Giuffre in London. Maxwell purportedly assumed the role of a personal aide to Epstein, and together they relocated between various locations such as New York, secluded residences in Palm Beach and New Mexico, and a private

Caribbean island called Little Saint James. During this period, they were frequently seen in the company of notable individuals, including Bill Clinton and renowned attorney Alan Dershowitz. According to federal authorities, Maxwell and Epstein collaborated between 1994 and 2004 to find young girls, prepare them for illicit activities, and subsequently persuade them to travel and be transported to Epstein's residences.

Conversely, it is claimed that Maxwell indulged in a "sumptuous existence" where she was attended to by her own dedicated personnel. Maxwell was also given a townhouse in New York City by Epstein, which he purchased for her. Additionally, Epstein transferred a sum of around $23 million to Maxwell throughout the duration of their illegal activities. Prosecutors additionally asserted that Maxwell cultivated an environment of secrecy at Epstein's houses, directing domestic staff to refrain from observing, hearing, or disclosing any information unless specifically prompted. The U.S. Attorney's Office for the Southern District of New York did not pursue the forfeiture of any real estate held by Maxwell, as the offenses in question were committed at Epstein's homes rather than any properties owned by Maxwell herself.

Eight women who allege that Maxwell exerted control and mistreated them over an extended period of time have submitted victim impact statements to the court for consideration in determining Maxwell's penalty. A few of them directed their thoughts towards the judge, but others communicated directly with Maxwell. Multiple individuals reported that their perpetrators eroded their self-confidence and inflicted profound harm by exploiting their young age and naivety.

The victims recounted their experiences of suppressing traumatic memories for an extended period, only to witness their resurgence in their later years. They detailed the persistent struggle of seeking justice against an individual who adamantly refuses to express regret. Similar to Maxwell in 1991, Epstein was also experiencing a loss of everything at the time of his death.

CHAPTER THREE

Allegations, Arrest and Death of Jeffery Epstein

Epstein faced his initial allegations of sexual molestation in Palm Beach in 2005. A woman reported to the police that her stepdaughter had been subjected to abuse by an affluent individual named Jeff. The Federal

Bureau of Investigation (FBI) quickly became involved. Additional allegations emerged, and when U.S. attorney Alexander Acosta, who later served as the secretary of labor under President Trump, initiated the process of building a criminal case, the number of purported victims had grown to approximately 40. Ultimately, although an abundance of evidence, the government reached a plca agreement in 2008 that resulted in Epstein serving a mere 13 months in prison. After being released, Maxwell and Epstein ceased to appear together in public, and she redirected her focus towards ecology, participating in conferences worldwide. Several civil lawsuits were filed against Epstein in the years following the plea agreement. Ms Giuffre initiated a civil lawsuit against Epstein in January 2015. The plaintiff claimed that Maxwell introduced her to Epstein under the false pretense of hiring her as a masseuse, but in reality, Epstein intended to groom her for sexual activities. Additionally, the plaintiff accused Maxwell of facilitating the recruitment and trafficking of other underage girls for the same purpose. Maxwell refuted the allegations and faced a lawsuit from Ms. Giuffre for defamation. The latter was victorious in her legal battle, compelling Maxwell to make a significant compensation payment in May 2017.

Maxwell clandestinely entered into matrimony during this period, marrying a technology tycoon. Scott Borgerson, the founder of CargoMetrics, a company specializing in maritime analytics, they kept their relationship hidden from the public until it was revealed in December 2020. A significant number of individuals were subjected to mistreatment at his extensive estate located on Little Saint James, his privately-owned island in the U.S. Virgin

Islands. Epstein utilized his wealth and power to evade a two-year investigation conducted by the Federal Bureau of Investigation (F.B.I.), ultimately admitting guilt to only two state crimes related to soliciting prostitution, one of which included a juvenile. On this occasion, though, he found himself ensnared. In July, federal prosecutors from the Southern District of New York charged him with orchestrating a sex-trafficking operation that exploited numerous teenage females. The judge rejected his request for bail. Additional witnesses emerged, and the case garnered immense prominence. Almost all individuals connected to Epstein abandoned him, including Leslie Wexner, the affluent retailer who seemingly played a crucial role in Epstein's financial success.

At the age of sixty-six, Epstein was confronted with the possibility of enduring an extended period of time in a dreadful prison that had previously held notorious figures such as John Gotti and El Chapo. He would have to confront his accusers in a criminal trial, potentially lose his wealth in civil lawsuits, and spend the remainder of his life in a federal penitentiary, without the privilege of work release that he had been granted during his initial imprisonment.

Epstein committed suicide in his cell at the Metropolitan Correctional Center on Saturday morning, and there is no evidence of any other individuals being implicated. This explanation is unsatisfactory in several aspects and prompts significant inquiries regarding the lack of closer supervision of Epstein.

Epstein's legal representatives were the ones who made the request for him to be removed from suicide watch. In violation of the norms and procedures of the Metropolitan Correctional Center and the Bureau of Prisons, Epstein was permitted to sleep on the floor and was provided with additional blankets and clothing. Prior to his death, Epstein was granted unsupervised access to a jail phone, which was a breach of BOP regulations. Additionally, despite his earlier suicide attempt, he was not given a new cellmate. Epstein was also expected to be under surveillance for his previous suicide attempt. However, two correctional guards, who were specifically tasked with overseeing Epstein during the night, neglected to do over 75 required inspections on him.

The individual remained in his confinement throughout the night and was only found deceased at 6:30 a.m. on August 10th.

Maxwell's Arrest and Sentencing

Following Epstein's apprehension, Maxwell evaded detection, exclusively dealing with the judicial system via her legal representatives. Following that, her agents initiated a court action in the Superior Court of the US Virgin Islands on 12 March 2020 against Jeffrey Epstein's estate, seeking to recover her incurred legal expenses. The FBI successfully apprehended and detained her on 2 July at a residence in Bradford, New Hampshire, after tracing her mobile phone. Maxwell faced charges of soliciting juveniles, engaging in child sex trafficking, and committing perjury. She denied all three counts. The trial was tentatively set for July 12, 2021. A federal judge in the Southern District of New York refused to grant her bail on July 14, determining that she posed a risk of fleeing. This decision was reaffirmed during a second bail application on December 28. By that time, Maxwell was believed to possess assets worth $22.5 million and had allocated around $7 million to fund her legal defense.

On January 25, 2021, her legal representatives contended that the charges against her were a "hodgepodge" and should be dismissed due to their failure to specify an accuser or provide a date for the alleged commission of a particular offense. After a span of 48 hours, a total of 112 legal documents pertaining to her case, which collectively consisted of numerous pages, were disclosed to the public. Notably, one statement said that Maxwell instructed a group of young girls to engage in sexual activities such as kissing, dancing, and touching each other, while the defendant and Epstein observed.

The documents also indicated that in a deposition given in 2016, she claimed to have no prior awareness of Epstein's actions and only became aware of them through the media. She stated that she learned about it "like everyone else, like the rest of the world, when it was announced in the newspapers."

Additionally, she mentioned that she stopped working for him because she was no longer content in her position. In March 2021, prosecutors in the Southern District of New York brought out two more allegations against Maxwell in their sex trafficking case. These charges specifically accuse her of engaging in a conspiracy to commit sex trafficking and of engaging in sex trafficking involving a juvenile. The supplementary indictment expands the period of Maxwell's purported participation in Epstein's exploitation of underage women to 2004, and introduces an additional claimed victim referred to as "Minor Victim-4." The prior indictment solely included occurrences spanning from 1994 to 1997. Maxwell refuted all allegations made against her and entered a plea of not guilty to all six federal charges. Throughout the trial, Maxwell was detained at the Metropolitan Detention Center in Brooklyn, New York. During her time there, she claimed to have been physically assaulted by a guard in February 2021 and expressed dissatisfaction with the harsh conditions she was subjected to. These conditions included frequent searches, constant surveillance, and being awakened every

15 minutes with a flashlight while sleeping, presumably to prevent any potential suicide attempt similar to Epstein's. Several adult women who were formerly girls testified throughout the trial, courageously revealing the extensive abuse they endured when Maxwell and Epstein lured them into their circle. Both individuals frequently used the appeal of riches and their associations with influential others, like Prince Andrew, Bill Clinton, and Donald Trump. Maxwell was recommended a 20-year sentence by the U.S. Probation Department, in accordance with federal guidelines for crimes characterized as

"heinous and predatory." However, the prosecutors requested a sentence ranging from 30 to 55 years, based on the significant number of victims and Maxwell's inability to accept accountability. Maxwell displayed minimal response as the verdicts were pronounced. Maxwell was observed pouring herself a glass of water and consuming it in little increments as the reading was taking place. Subsequently, she was escorted out of the courthouse by marshals without any restraints, and was taken back to the Metropolitan Detention Centre where she will remain until her sentencing hearing.

Maxwell's legal team promptly initiated the process of appealing her case and simultaneously filed a distinct motion for a new trial. This decision was prompted by the disclosure of one of the initial jurors who, in an interview with the media, admitted to having a personal background involving sexual assault. The defense argued that Juror 50, provided false information about his background during the pre-trial proceedings, leading to an unjust trial. However, Judge Alison Nathan finally dismissed their request for a new trial.

CHAPTER FOUR

Harvey Weinstein's Early Life and Career

Harvey Weinstein, an American film producer, was born on March 19, 1952, in Flushing, Queens, New York, U.S. He, together with his brother Bob, served as the co-founder and co-chairman of Miramax Films from 1979 to 2005, and later the Weinstein Company from 2005 to 2017. Formerly a prominent figure in the entertainment industry, his professional trajectory came to an abrupt halt as a result of multiple accusations of sexual harassment and assault, some of which resulted in legal charges and subsequent convictions.

Harvey Weinstein and his younger brother, Bob, were raised in Queens as amicable yet fierce rivals. Max, their father, was a reserved and corpulent individual employed as a diamond cutter in Manhattan. Miriam, their mother, managed the household.

Weinstein enrolled at the University of Buffalo, New York, where he initiated the promotion of rock concerts alongside his brother. In 1979, the brothers founded the Miramax Film Corp., named after their parents Miriam and Max. They swiftly shifted their focus to the film industry, acquiring film rights and distributing them. Weinstein shown a propensity for taking risks by acquiring films that were unconventional and frequently generated controversy. In 1989, he acquired the rights to the provocative picture sex, lies, and videotape, which subsequently became Miramax's inaugural blockbuster.

In the early 1990s, the company expanded its influence as the brothers increased their film production. Harvey, who possessed a more extravagant and sociable personality, emerged as the public representative of Miramax. The Walt Disney Company acquired the company in 1993 for an approximate sum of $60 million, while the brothers remained as cochairmen. Subsequently, a series of highly regarded films were released. In 1997, Weinstein and Miramax achieved their inaugural Academy Award for best picture with The English Patient (1996). Weinstein produced a collection of immensely prosperous movies. For many years, there circulated reports in the Hollywood industry regarding Harvey Weinstein's sexual misconduct towards women. In order to quash such narratives, he frequently utilized the same techniques he employed to promote his movies, which garnered a total of eighty-one Academy Awards (along with three hundred and forty-one nominations): a substantial network of contacts and an assertive and coercive manner. His techniques proved effective over an extended period of time. The individuals who accused him were rendered silent. Actors and directors competed for the opportunity to participate in his movies, agencies yielded to his requests, and the press praised the majority of the pictures he produced. Bill and Hillary Clinton were present at his premieres.

As Miramax transitioned from a distributor to a mini-studio, generating over $1 billion in annual box-office revenue, Weinstein started to establish the company as an entertainment empire. In 1998, a television section was established, and the subsequent year saw the birth of Talk magazine, a collaboration with Hearst Publishing, in various retail outlets. Talk Miramax Books was founded in the year 2000. Despite the challenges faced by the new initiatives, there was a belief that Weinstein's divided attention was negatively impacting the film division, resulting in Miramax receiving only one Academy Award in 2002. In 2003, Weinstein's films garnered 40 Academy Award nominations, surpassing any other studio in over six decades. Ultimately, these films secured 9 prizes, including the prestigious best picture accolade for Chicago (2002).

The Allegations

Allegations of decades-long sexual harassment and assault against Harvey Weinstein first surfaced in October 2017. He was let go from the Weinstein Company just days after taking a leave of absence. Not long after that, he was kicked out of the National Academy of Motion Pictures. Weinstein was subject to many charges, including rape, stemming from incidents involving two separate women in May 2018 after a probe by New York authorities. Not guilty pleas were entered by Weinstein on those and other accusations that were later brought against him.

Weinstein was involved in other court battles. Between 2004 and 2013, he faced four rape and assault charges in California. He was convicted guilty of rape, forcible oral sex, and sexual penetration in a Los Angeles jury's 2022 trial. The charges stemmed from an event that occurred in 2013 involving an Italian actress. On the other hand, the jury either found Weinstein not guilty or deadlocked on the accusations against his other accusers.

Weinstein has also been the target of allegations of sexual assault and harassment for over 20 years. Many people in Hollywood and elsewhere have known about his actions. The four male board members of the Weinstein Company resigned and Weinstein was fired after a damning report surfaced several sexual harassments claims against him on October 5th.

Dozens of prominent men were accused of sexual misconduct, sacked or forced to quit in the months following the public disclosure of the allegations against Weinstein. The results were noticeable right away for Weinstein. The

Weinstein Company board of directors sacked him on October 8th, with his brother Bob casting the deciding vote. According to Weinstein, who testified before the board, the press accounts were inaccurate and the intercourse had been voluntary. In a statement he released to the public, he admitted simply that he struggled with controlling his rage. It didn't take long for Weinstein to lose membership in the Oscars, an honorary doctorate from his alma college, the University at Buffalo, and the French Legion of Honor, despite his denials. Weinstein had been fighting back for years, and he was still determined to do so.

CHAPTER FIVE

An Over-Stretched Trial

In early 2018, anticipating an impending indictment, Weinstein scheduled a lunch meeting with New York attorney Benjamin Brafman. Having been born in Brooklyn to parents who survived the Holocaust, Brafman, much like Weinstein, attended a public educational institution and saw himself as a resilient individual of

Jewish descent. He has previously acted as legal counsel for another individual accused of sexual misconduct, specifically a French economist and politician. The accusations against this individual were likewise dismissed by Vance's office due to concerns about the reliability of the alleged victim. Although he had reservations about Brafman's hourly fee of $1500, he was swayed by Brafman's prestigious title as the city's "Best Criminal Defense Lawyer" and ultimately retained him as his defense attorney.

During that spring, Weinstein attempted to get Brafman to facilitate a meeting with Vance and Governor Andrew Cuomo. He desired that Vance could be persuaded to eliminate the potential indictment. Brafman held the belief that this scheme was destined for failure, and confidently reassured Weinstein that he possessed the ability to secure victory in the event of a trial. However, as per multiple reports, Weinstein persisted in seeking the meeting.

Weinstein was instructed to present himself to the First Precinct station house of the New York Police Department in lower Manhattan on the morning of May 25, 2018. Weinstein, accompanied by Brafman, was greeted by a group of reporters and photographers who were positioned behind metal barricades. They directed inquiries towards him as he proceeded forward. The individual was apprehended and formally accused of committing first- and third-degree rape, as well as engaging in a criminal sexual act of the highest degree. The charges implicated two women, subsequently identified as Jessica Mann, an aspiring actress, and Lucia Evans, a college student who also harbored aspirations of becoming an actor. Weinstein departed the station with his hands restrained behind his back and was accompanied to the Criminal Courthouse on Centre Street, where he was instructed to provide a bond amount of one million dollars. A metallic tracking device was securely attached to his right ankle, and he surrendered his passport, consenting to limit his travel to New York and Connecticut.

The prosecution contended that Weinstein had exploited his authority as the leader of Miramax, and subsequently of the Weinstein Company, to ensnare actresses, models, and other women in the entertainment business. Following his forceful coercion of women, often employing cruel methods, to engage in sexual activities with him, he ensured their silence by pressuring them to sign non-disclosure agreements (N.D.A.s) or by threatening to undermine their professional endeavors.

Brafman aimed to establish that the accusers had given their consent to engage in sexual activity with Weinstein, and he sought to support this claim by highlighting the ongoing ties they maintained with him. He aimed to depict Weinstein as a man who was influenced and controlled by women who were keen on exploiting his influence to advance their professional pursuits. Furthermore, he contended, employing terminology from a different time period, that "Mr. Weinstein was not the originator of the practice known as the casting couch." Brafman pointed out that the purported offenses were never officially reported to the authorities. Additionally, there were no supporting witnesses, and no scientific proof such as forensic or DNA analysis to establish Weinstein's culpability. However, even if Brafman managed to convince a jury in New York to declare his client innocent, Weinstein still had the possibility of facing criminal proceedings in Los Angeles, London, and Dublin. He faced numerous civil claims from women alleging sexual abuse. In contrast to a criminal case, where jurors must be convinced of the defendant's guilt "beyond a reasonable doubt," a civil lawsuit usually just requires a "preponderance of evidence" to establish the defendant's liability.

Justice James Burke, a former Assistant District Attorney in Manhattan with twelve years of experience, was randomly chosen to preside over the case, which is being heard at the State Supreme Court. The indictment alleged that Weinstein coerced Lucia Evans into engaging in oral sexual activity with him. Subsequently, the prosecution uncovered that a detective had deliberately concealed evidence pertaining to Evans's statement, prompting both parties to request her removal from the indictment. Justice Burke consented to dismiss Evans from the lawsuit. Weinstein acknowledged Brafman with a nod from the defense table. Subsequently, he discovered that the ruling made by the Justice would result in financial consequences for him. As the purported incident involving Evans occurred in 2004, during the period when Miramax was under the ownership of the Walt Disney Company,

Disney's insurance was responsible for covering Weinstein's legal expenses. However, the episodes involving Mann took place after the departure of the Weinstein brothers from Miramax in 2005, when they established the Weinstein Company. Weinstein was now responsible for covering all of his legal expenses out of his own pocket.

Brafman submitted multiple motions to dismiss the case, however, on December 20, 2018, Justice Burke upheld the indictment. Brafman expressed his unwavering confidence in the trial's success. While Weinstein and Brafman maintained a unified public image, they had been engaged in a prolonged dispute over the specifics of the defense strategy. Disregarding the counsel of his lawyer, Weinstein maintained that his defense team must engage with the media and employ a female attorney who would mitigate his public perception prior to the jurors. Brafman was fatigued at the end of the year. He informed a colleague that Harvey is a challenging individual, seemingly more challenging than certain criminals he had previously defended. Several weeks later, Brafman informed Justice Burke of his intention to resign as Weinstein's attorney. Both he and Weinstein released public statements asserting that the separation was "amicable."

In January 2019, Weinstein enlisted the services of two prominent attorneys: Jose Baez, a renowned lawyer from Florida with a track record of handling high-profile cases, and Ronald S. Sullivan, Jr., a distinguished professor at Harvard Law School. The team consisted of Duncan Levin, a former federal and New York state prosecutor, and Arthur Aidala, a Brooklyn native who provided legal advice to both Anthony Weiner, the former New York congressman, and Roger Ailes, the former CEO of Fox News, in relation to allegations of sexual misconduct.

Weinstein believed he had assembled an exceptional group of individuals that would be attractive to jurors in the city. The duration did not exceed six months. Sullivan was the first to depart, leaving on May 10th due to substantial teaching obligations. In 2009, Sullivan achieved the distinction of becoming the inaugural Black individual to be selected as a faculty dean at Harvard College. He assumed the leadership role at Winthrop House, which is a residential facility for undergraduate students. A multitude of students vehemently condemned his advocacy for Weinstein and demanded his immediate resignation from the position of dean. Despite the fact that most of the faculty at the law school signed a petition in support of Sullivan, they announced on May 13th that Sullivan will not be reappointed as dean. They clarified that his departure was not only due to his representation of Weinstein.

Baez departed in June, subsequent to composing a strongly critical letter to Justice Burke, elucidating that Weinstein had issued a threat to file a lawsuit against his legal establishment. Weinstein selected the Chicago-based attorney Donna Rotunno to spearhead his defense. Rotunno, a former prosecutor, proudly claimed to have successfully defended forty sex-crime cases, with only one loss. She informed the reporters that her gender provided her with a benefit when questioning women during cross-examination. Rotunno was accompanied by Damon Cheronis, a fellow law school graduate who is highly skilled in criminal law. Aidala was the last remaining member from Weinstein's prior staff.

In August 2019, Justice Burke authorized the prosecution to summon three Molineux witnesses. These individuals would provide testimony regarding occurrences not specifically mentioned in the indictment, which might potentially demonstrate behavioral patterns shown by the defendant or corroborate the allegations made by the accusers. Weinstein's attorneys vehemently objected against the admission of these witnesses, recognizing that their testimony could be particularly detrimental if presented to the jury. The Molineux witnesses in the Weinstein trial consist of three aspiring actresses: Lauren Young, Dawn Dunning, and Tarale Wulff. All three of them have accused Weinstein of assaulting them.

Justice Burke, in addition to the defense's setback, permitted testimony from Miriam Haley, previously known as Mimi Haleyi, a production assistant, and the actress Annabella Sciorra, both of whom had previously appeared before a grand jury in July. Haley accused Weinstein of sexually assaulting her at his SoHo apartment in 2006, among other allegations. Sciorra provided testimony stating that Weinstein sexually assaulted her by engaging in non-consensual sexual intercourse at her residence in Gramercy Park during the early 1990s. A new indictment was returned by the grand jury, containing five accusations including predatory sexual assault and rape in the first degree. The charges pertain to three women: Jessica Mann, Miriam Haley, and Annabella Sciorra.

Procedural Inquiries and Jury Compilations

The trial of Weinstein commenced on January 6, 2020, in 100 Centre Street, located in the southern part of Manhattan. Over the course of the following eight weeks, Weinstein consistently attended court hearings wearing unremarkable, ill-fitting suits. His attire consisted of plain white shirts with wrinkled collars and uninteresting neckties. His health had declined. Since the claims emerged, he dropped a significant amount of weight. Additionally, his facial hair was uneven, with stubble visible on his face. The first day was primarily focused on procedural inquiries. On the second day, Justice Burke entered in a state of anger. A security officer observed Weinstein engaging in texting, which is a breach of the court's regulations. Burke inquired the defendant, "Is this truly the manner in which you desire to be incarcerated for the remainder of your existence?"

One factor the defense considered while choosing the jury was to specifically target older individuals, both men and women, who may be more inclined to sympathize with someone from Weinstein's age group. Ultimately, the jury panel comprised six Caucasian males, two Caucasian females, three African-American females, and one African-American male, who assumed the role of the jury foreman. Both sides appeared to be evenly matched without any discernible edge.

Weinstein was typically accompanied by Rotunno and his four other attorneys, positioned at a table directly across from Justice Burke. The prosecutors, namely Illuzzi, the Assistant District Attorney, and her assistant, Meghan Hast, were positioned at a table adjacent to Burke's right side, in close proximity to the jury box.

Illuzzi relinquished control of the opening arguments to Hast, who directed attention towards Weinstein. "The individual positioned on that particular side of the courtroom, regardless of the visual perception of your eyes, is not an innocuous elderly gentleman," she stated. By using a remote device, she displayed an image on two expansive displays depicting a radiant Weinstein beside Bill Clinton. She characterized the accused as a prominent Hollywood producer leading an extravagant lifestyle, who engaged in a dual career as a predator, subjecting these victims to sexual abuse when they resisted his demands and commands. Hast presented images of each woman and detailed the impact that Weinstein's acts of aggression had inflicted upon them. In order to proactively address a possible weakness in the prosecution's argument, she stated her intention to provide testimony from a forensic psychiatrist to debunk misconceptions about rape, such as the notion that victims do not maintain contact with their assailants. Hast also argued that certain workers of Weinstein played a role in facilitating his acts of abuse. The woman claimed that female employees escorted people to Weinstein's hotel suites, and he utilized these staff members to deceive victims into feeling safe before being left alone with him.

Following Hast's presentation, Cheronis, Weinstein's attorney, confidently walked in front of the jury box, nonchalantly mentioning the names of Weinstein's accusers. He presented the identical argument as Weinstein's previous attorneys, asserting that these interactions were consensual. Cheronis cautioned the jurors against reaching a guilty verdict for Weinstein solely on the basis of media coverage or the assumption that all women's statements must be accepted as true. He asserted that upon examining the evidence, specifically an email from Jessica Mann to Weinstein that stated, "Miss you big guy," they should question whether it is plausible for a woman to compose such an affectionate message to her rapist. According to him, jurors were required to hold women responsible for their actions.

Starting from the spring of 2017, Weinstein had concerns that Annabella Sciorra and other women were divulging unfavorable accounts about him to the media. He had engaged the services of a covert security agency, to conduct surveillance on them. Sciorra was the initial witness called by the prosecution.

During the direct examination conducted by Illuzzi, Sciorra testified that she had attended a Miramax dinner in New York in either late 1993 or early 1994. At the time, she was 33 years old and had recently played a leading role in one of Weinstein's films, a romantic comedy depicting the lives of three individuals residing in the same apartment in Greenwich Village, but on different days. Upon her departure from the dinner, Weinstein extended the opportunity to provide transportation to her residence, located in Gramercy Park. She accompanied him on the journey back to her residence and bid farewell. However, later that evening, she was abruptly surprised by a sudden rap on her door. Sciorra alleged that "the defendant" forcefully opened the door and swiftly moved past her, meticulously examining each room, presumably to ascertain the absence of any other individuals. He commenced the action of taking off his shirt and disregarded her requests for him to depart. He forcefully pushed her into the bed. "I was striking him with my fists and feet," she recollected, yet he surpassed her in weight by over one hundred and fifty pounds. Sciorra alleges that Weinstein forcefully mounted her, restrained her hands, and sexually assaulted her. Subsequently, he uttered the words, "This is intended for you," and proceeded to engage in oral stimulation.

Sciorra described the experience as like a seizure. Weinstein discreetly rose from the bed and departed the apartment.

Illuzzi inquired about her subsequent actions.

"I desired to feign that it never occurred," Sciorra remarked. She ceased her employment and starting using alcohol excessively. Upon receiving an invitation from a friend to attend another Miramax dinner, she accepted with the intention of directly addressing Weinstein. During her testimony, she stated that he cautioned her during the event, saying, "This information must remain confidential between us." She further stated, "It was highly intimidating." His eyes turned completely black.

The defense was aware that cross-examination would pose challenges. Sciorra's evidence had captivated the jurors, and her responses had been succinct, providing little opportunities for rebuttal. Rotunno stepped to the lectern and inquired why Sciorra hadn't called the police.

"During that period, I lacked the comprehension that the incident constituted rape," Sciorra responded.

Prior to this, she had expressed her belief that rape was a crime typically occurring in a secluded area, perpetrated by an unfamiliar individual. Rotunno persistently questioned Sciorra, seeking any discrepancies in her account. By what means did Weinstein acquire knowledge of her apartment number? What was the reason for her inability to recall the precise month and year in which the rape took place? Did she subsequently disclose to her friend Paul Feldsher, the producer, that she engaged in consenting sexual activity with Weinstein? Sciorra declined the last inquiry, responding in a composed manner.

Next, two acquaintances of Sciorra were subjected to cross-examination. During her testimony, actress Rosie Perez stated that Sciorra had confided in her over the phone, saying, "I believe something unfortunate occurred to me." I believe that constituted a case of sexual assault. However, she had declined to disclose the perpetrator's identity. Upon Perez's subsequent speculation that Weinstein was the perpetrator, she urged Sciorra to file a formal complaint over the incident. According to her, Sciorra responded by saying, "I am unable to do so because he will ruin my professional life."

Aidala interrogated Kara Young, a model, about Sciorra's consumption of alcohol and self-inflicted damage, causing her to become progressively distressed. Aidala spoke for length, prompting Justice Burke to instruct him to conclude his remarks. Justice Burke then excused Young from the courtroom, who departed while visibly upset.

Miriam Haley was called to testify on January 27th. She recounted encountering Weinstein in 2004, during a film premiere in London, then encountering him once more, two years later, at Cannes. There, Weinstein extended an invitation to her to join him in his hotel suite. She desired employment; he requested a massage. Haley declined, however, at a later juncture, they shared contact details and maintained communication. After several months, she gave a sworn statement that he extended an invitation for her to visit his loft located in SoHo. Upon her arrival, she reported that he made an attempt to seize her, forcefully propelled her into the bedroom, and proceeded to remove her garments.

During her testimony, she stated that she loudly exclaimed she was menstruation. According to her account, he restrained her, removed her tampon forcefully, and inserted his tongue into her vagina. Her recollection of the assault was so vivid that she remembered the children's illustrations on the wall of the room. On the day of the attack, Haley recounted that she informed a roommate about the incident, but refrained from contacting the police. After several weeks, Weinstein extended an invitation to her for beverages at the Tribeca Grand Hotel, and she agreed. She was instructed to proceed to Weinstein's apartment. Upon entering the room, she recounted that Weinstein forcibly pulled her onto the bed, causing her to experience a state of numbness as he engaged in non-consensual sexual activity with her.

In anticipation of the defense's interrogative approach, Hast inquired about the reasons behind Haley's continued communication with Weinstein. Haley recollected that the initial occurrence was profoundly humiliating. Following the second occurrence, I held myself responsible. She subsequently expressed, "I simply stored it in a box, as though it never occurred." In her opening remarks, Hast noted that Haley seemed to be attempting to "nearly standardize the situation."

During the cross-examination, Cheronis interpreted these statements as an admission that the relationship was consensual. He presented an email in which Haley requested Weinstein to arrange her transportation to Los Angeles; she affixed her signature to another communication. "Lots of love." Cheronis inquired about whether he made advances towards you during the initial massage request. If that was the case, why did you continue to maintain contact with him? "I required employment," she stated. A grand total of twenty-eight witnesses were summoned by the prosecution. During every legal proceeding, attorneys endeavor to construct a compelling storyline by employing impactful specifics, thought-provoking inquiries, and memorable introductory and concluding statements. Weinstein has demonstrated his proficiency in narrative craftsmanship inside the film industry. However, trials differ from movies as they are not filmed in controlled environments and modified during the post-production process. Occasionally, a trial might be defined by a single witness or even a solitary moment.

Observers familiar with Weinstein were astounded by his very feeble appearance during the court proceedings. What was even more surprising was his seeming passivity, as he appeared aloof and only partially engaged in his own trial, as his accusers detailed his body odor, his pimpled physique, and his malformed genitals. In order to validate the accuracy of the physical descriptions provided by his accusers, the prosecution secured a legal authorization mandating him to assume a state of nudity for the purpose of being photographed. Five of these images were then presented to the jury, who expeditiously circulated them during the court proceedings.

CHAPTER FIVE

The Jury's Verdict and Weinstein's Sentencing

The jury said that it had arrived at a verdict. Vance, the District Attorney, promptly arrived from his adjacent office within a matter of minutes. The defendant, accompanied by his buddy William Currao, was flanked by four Supreme Court officers wearing protective vests. The jurors arrived in the courtroom shortly before midday.

Bernard Cody, the leader of the jury, stood forward to declare the verdict. Weinstein was convicted on count two, which pertains to a criminal sexual act involving Haley, and count five, which pertains to third-degree rape involving Mann. The court clerk conducted a numerical poll of the jurors. Every juror, without of any sign of emotion, affirmed the decision of guilt.

Justice Burke issued an order for Weinstein to be transferred to Rikers Island. The recommendation was made for him to be admitted to the medical unit of the jail due to his ongoing recovery from a back procedure. After being placed in a car to Rikers Island, Weinstein was struck by chest symptoms; his blood pressure jumped up. He was redirected to the prisoner ward at Bellevue Hospital, where a stent was surgically placed in a coronary artery to prevent obstructions. After the passage of one week, he was relocated to Rikers.

Weinstein was sent to the Wende Correctional Facility, a high-security state prison of fifteen acres, located twenty miles east of Buffalo. He was admitted to the hospital ward, where he had his own individual cell but shared meals in a communal mess hall with other patients. He was granted three hours of daily release from his confinement. His Internet access was refused and he was only allowed to make calls to a limited number of preapproved contacts, which included his two youngest children and his lawyers.

Weinstein persisted in his aspiration to overturn his criminal conviction in New York. His lawyers submitted an appeal on April 5, 2021, based on the argument that Justice Burke's biased decisions compromised the fairness of the trial. These decisions include allowing Molineux witnesses to testify, which potentially violated the defendant's

Sixth Amendment right to be tried only on charges brought by a Grand Jury. Additionally, the failure to dismiss Juror No. 11, who had written a novel about young women involved in relationships with older men, denied Weinstein's right to a trial by an unbiased jury. Both parties are unaware of the anticipated ruling date from the appeals court.

Closing Remark

The accounts of Harvey Weinstein, Jeffrey Epstein, and Ghislaine Maxwell are intricately interwoven, unveiling distinct aspects of power abuse, exploitation, and a shadowy realm beneath influential organizations. The broader societal concerns that are reflected in the conclusions drawn from their respective cases are the complexities of addressing sexual abuse, the power dynamics of privilege, and the significance of holding individuals accountable irrespective of their social standing. The case involving Jeffrey Epstein demonstrated the degree to which individuals with connections and affluence could evade legal consequences. The pardon he was granted in his initial plea agreement of 2008 drew attention to systemic deficiencies within the legal system, inciting widespread public indignation and calls for reform. Numerous inquiries remained unresolved following his arrest and demise in 2019, underscoring the intricate nature of seeking justice in situations involving influential individuals.

The purported participation of Ghislaine Maxwell in Epstein's sex trafficking operations drew attention to the complicity of certain individuals in facilitating such heinous acts. Her apprehension and the trial that followed demonstrated the significance of investigating those who facilitate exploitation and trafficking by indicating a shift toward holding accomplices accountable.

The conviction and high-profile trial of Harvey Weinstein represented a turning point in the #MeToo movement. The conviction of Harvey Weinstein, a prominent Hollywood producer, for rape and sexual assault signified a significant shift in the entertainment sector. The trial underscored the importance of providing a forum for survivors to confront their abusers and dismantling the longstanding culture of silence that had shielded offenders.

When viewed within a wider framework, these instances emphasize the critical nature of confronting the imbalances of power that enable sexual misconduct to persist. These findings emphasize the necessity for comprehensive reforms in corporate, legal, and cultural spheres to foster an environment where survivors are encouraged to report abuse and where offenders, irrespective of social standing, are held accountable for their conduct.

END

www.ingramcontent.com/pod-product-compliance
Lightning Source LLC
Chambersburg PA
CBHW070857260726
48661CB00004B/1466